Bounce Back Better

Bounce Back Better

How to WIN After Great LOSS

MAYA W TYLER

ISBN: 1515220893
ISBN 13: 9781515220893
Library of Congress Control Number: 2015912086
CreateSpace Independent Publishing Platform
North Charleston, South Carolina

Table of Contents

Dedication

I dedicate this to the strongest, most influential women I know: Doctor Susan Bernstein, my therapist, rest in peace you beautiful, life changing woman. Doctor Tujuana Patterson White, my mom and hero; and to Doctor Paulette W. Johnson, my coach and my "mom away from home" during the crazy college years.

And to my Daddy. For bringing me home when I'd felt the whole world had tossed me out, and showing me strength and unwavering stability when I needed it most.

A Note:

Dear Reader,

This is not your typical self-help book. Needing help to recover from any loss usually follows a sobering, negative, stressful situation, and is not a matter that should be taken lightly. However, from my perspective, gloomy, somber textbooks did not fit me, nor could I just write that way with the hope of motivating someone who is already experiencing grief and depression. So, since I have been through it myself, I decided to add my own flavor.

Being a survivor of the hell and havoc that loss can inflict on even the most positive people, it wouldn't be ME if I tried to write this without a little color, a few smiles, and sprinklings of random humor. I also know I do not have the attention span to sit through an entire non-fiction book without some sort of stimulation for the other side of my brain, so I will not make you do that, either. ☺ Sometimes we need more than just words; strategically placed throughout this book, there will be questions, pictures, and even a few fun activities to stimulate your brain to help you visualize and physically map out your plan of attack to bounce back! Please feel free to write right in the book or write along in your own journal to answer the questions or to complete an activity.

I wish you the very best of luck on your journey as well as peace and healing for your soul.

-Maya Tyler

Forward

I am not by any means perfect—not before my story began and not after. I do not claim to be miraculously different, holy, sanctified, or completely changed. I am a work in progress. My point in writing this book was not for me to "get this off my chest," nor to publicly perform a grand piteous party for my own solace, nor is it a sappy, sobbing book that only talks about the grief. There is a tremendous spirit of inspiration, love, and overcoming in addition to a little humor, without which, God knows I would not have made it this far. There is no happy ending, at least not yet. There *is* new love, new life, and optimistic new beginnings. Though I hope it proves to be therapeutic, my purpose for telling my story of overcoming grief, anxiety, depression, and pain is simple: to help someone else.

Throughout this book I include parts of my journey and go over the things that I believe made me the woman I am today. I am proud of who I have become in the wake of tragedy. I am proud of my struggle, my process, my blessings, and my progress. Most of all, I am proud of everything it took for me to bounce back, and be better.

Part 1 – Accept

One

MY STORY

*T*he day he died, we were having one of those days. We argued a little, kissed and made up, and marveled at how much two people could be in love at such a young age. It happened pretty often actually in the 10 years we had together, when we would look at each other and wholly appreciate the experience to really be in love. In fact, we had even danced randomly, to no music at all, just a few hours before he had fallen in a relay race. He struck his head on a rock in the ground. About 30 minutes later, he was unconscious, and would never open his eyes again.

It was Easter Sunday and we were out in King William, Virginia. The country, they call it; way out in the sticks. His aunt's house had this huge, beautiful yard; the kids were having an Easter egg hunt and playing games in it, while the mothers with the young babies were indoors. I was inside with my not-quite-walking one-year-old, chatting with relatives-- secretly relieved to not be outside playing-- but simultaneously guilty that, once again, Jason was. But he loved playing with the kids. Our oldest, Justin was (as usual) attached at his daddy's knees. The folks outside were all participating in what appeared to be a relay race, and they sounded like they were having a ball.

Suddenly, Justin came bursting into the house, hysterical and crying about someone who was "going to die." Justin was then, and is still, a very expressive little boy, and I figured he was just exaggerating someone's minor injury. I glanced out the window and sure enough, someone was lying on the ground. I mistook the person for Jason's cousin Tony, and assumed his wife would go out and tend to him if necessary, but no big deal. Yet Justin persisted. He kept saying it: "He's going to die," over and over again. A few seconds later, I asked him, "Who Justin? Who is going to die?" "DAD!" he said, with the gravest look on his 6-year old face I had ever seen. I got up immediately, asking my in-laws to please keep an eye on my children while I saw what the issue was.

As I got outside, I could see that Jason was on the ground and the look on his face was not one I had seen before. He was in a lot of pain and he wore a look of frustration and disbelief – as if he could not believe the pain was so intense and that it was not subsiding with time. Apparently, in the backwards relay race he had tripped over something, and landed back-of-the-head first onto a random piece of asphalt in the yard. He was losing a lot of blood and had a strained look, as if he knew something was really, *very* wrong. The ambulance had been called several times and at least a half hour had crept by, yet they had not arrived.

I held his hand and squeezed, telling him what came to mind instinctively—that he would be fine, and I was right there. His cousins were quizzing him jokingly, asking him how many fingers were being held up, who he was, and what his birthdate was. He had answered them all correctly. Jason's last intelligible words were the answer to the last question, which his cousin Kiragu had asked: His birthdate. November 3, 1977. It was in the next few minutes that I saw the things I was most afraid of happening. He began to die.

He seemed to pass out, his eyelids fluttering, and when his pupils dilated he began to snore loudly, eyes half open. I knew this meant he had lost consciousness, but then he began to foam at the mouth. This was the most terrifying thing I had ever seen and, for some reason, probably due to some TV show I saw in the past, I knew it meant he had lost connectivity to his brain. In forty minutes, the ambulance had yet to show. His family had begun trying to revive him, yet all the while I was thinking, "Why don't they know he's gone?"

I pulled my hand away from his, unable to remain silent in this horror show. I completely lost it. Crying and hysteria are just descriptive words… not accurately describing what "losing it" really meant for me in this case. I will say that it didn't look like I was ever going to find "it" again. I was watching myself in slow motion, and I was the only one who knew he was dying. It was like I was literally feeling him being torn from the earth, from my heart, and from our kids—our family… my life. I remember thinking aloud, in a bit of a hazy tearful moment: "My life does not work without him." The line came from a movie, *Jerry McGuire*, with Cuba Gooding and Tom Cruise, only I was not an actress and my husband was really dying. I had not meant to quote a movie at such an odd time, but it was the first thing that came to mind. I meant it with all of my heart.

Moment after excruciating moment, the thought that kept circling my mind was: *If he lives and has to be a vegetable, he will hate me. I know him. He would hate for his children to see him that way, to be sad, wishing he would wake up, wishing for his hugs and his able body. He would hate me and that would be a terrifying and horrible existence for him —and for me. He would know I suffered just to look at him there, unable to be a man for me, and he would hate himself. I cannot do that to him. I will have no choice but to pull the plug. Will I be able to do that?*

About an hour into this episode, the ambulance finally showed up. I wish now that I'd had the strength *then* to bring a huge lawsuit against them for taking so long. They took Jason's vitals and grimly put him into the ambulance. From the EMTs mouths there were half-hearted reassurances that they were doing everything possible, but their faces said differently. They knew something. I tried to get into the ambulance, but could not bear it. I could not watch him die. I climbed on, but something held me at the doors and my knees gave out from under me. Someone caught me. I could not bear being in that ambulance knowing what I would have to witness.

I still hold that guilt to this day. I should have held his hand. I should have been there with him, whatever was left of his mind died alone with strangers. And that is *my fault*. I followed behind in his mother's car, riding in the backseat, on the phone, tearfully recanting the story to my mom. She and my dad immediately jumped into their cars and were on their way to us from Maryland. I watched the paramedics through the glass windows in the back door of the ambulance as we followed behind them to the hospital. I watched as they scrambled about suddenly, appearing to administer a defibrillator… and then a few seconds later, they all calmly sat down. Just sitting, for the duration of the ride. I think I knew then what it meant. Mentally, however, I would not do more than stick a toe into that tidal wave. I was not ready.

When we finally arrived at a hospital that seemed further away than it should have been, the hospital staff wheeled Jason away with the sheet over his face, ushering me away when I tried to ask what was happening. I was told by an ambulance volunteer: "You can't be here, go to the waiting room."

The Hospital Floor

Three hours later, when the empty-headed (probably just exhausted) nurse entered our crowded waiting room and told us they were able to restart Jason's heart, my heart skipped a beat. A million emotions where crammed into that one second, my whole body had snapped to attention. I could feel again, the impossible hope that he would live and that this would all be a crazy story I blogged about tomorrow rose into my throat and I held my breath. In the next breath that bitch took, however, she retracted her words and corrected "able" to "UNABLE," meaning she had meant to say the doctors had been *unable* to restart his heart.

I had known all long he had died; I saw it. I felt it. I watched. I should have been inside the ambulance. I saw the sheet over him. I saw the people stop trying to save him. These thoughts, along with his mother's loud sorrowful reaction - like a physical blow to her heart that we all heard come through her mouth – and the whole room of people just reacting with moans and mumbles of disbelief, and then they piled onto me. I can remember feeling like I was getting smaller and I sank into the floor. I wanted to die. Not because of my immeasurable pain, not because of the shock or the sudden chunk of myself that was missing and never coming back. No, it was because of my kids and what I had to do now. Sitting on the floor amidst my swirling thoughts, I remember saying aloud the precise point of utter destruction for me: "What do I tell my babies?"

I fell onto the floor and wept. I sobbed about my children. What would I tell them? I sobbed about Jason's pain and how guilty I felt for not being able to stop it or get him help sooner or punish the ambulance for taking so long. I blamed myself for not being outside with him when it happened and not having more time to say goodbye. I sat in my shock about how fast it all happened and how crazy the situation was. I just sat there, on the hospital floor, unable to move because I *wanted to die.* The pain was unimaginably immense and I could not take it all in at once; each breath felt wasted, I would have given anything to give them to my husband instead. He was my best friend, my soul mate and my life partner in this crazy parenthood thing. Cliché as it sounds....it really *was* us against the world! He was my soldier and as I was recently diagnosed with anxiety disorder, he was my shield from the rest of the world, doing double duty to make up for my share of everything throughout the whole crazy ordeal. I negotiated with God about how He had made a mistake; He needed to take me instead because *Jason* was the better parent. I did not think I was fit to be a parent without him. Looking back, I think more than anything, the thing that nagged at me the most was having to be alone with the decisions we had fearlessly made together. Nothing was impossible, as long as we had each other.

Interrupting my thoughts, Nurse Bitch came over and said two incredibly stupid things that I will never forget. The first was, "Oh honey don't lay on the floor, this is a hospital and it's dirty." I'm going to take a deep breath here, telling this story, and choose, again, not to react to that. The second thing she said was: "How old are your babies"? Like it mattered! All I could think of was that they were good kids—really good, awesome kids and he was *their* phenomenal daddy. And I have to tell them now that he's dead and gone forever. They didn't deserve this.

That night I slept in the bed with my parents for the first time since I was a little kid. My sister tried to call me on my cell; she was, and still is, the only person on earth who could yank the composure right off my face with just her phone presence. I refused to speak to her, twice, and the third time all she had to say was hello. I was done. I could not talk. Pain was the only sound I had left in me. I was like that for days. Just unable to do much other than cry and blow my nose. I did not eat or sleep or take care of my baby much. I just sat.

In the following days, holding my baby was the only comfort I could find. I could not face Justin. Just the thought of him brought along with it a stabbing pain in my chest and a lump in my throat. I felt like it was my fault. He did not ask for this life, I gave it to him. The one thing he loved the most in this world, I had to be the one to tell him he would never see again. I will never, ever, forget what I had to say to him the morning after Jason died. He asked me, casually, "So when is Dad coming back?" He seemed only mildly concerned since he knew his dad to be indestructible and had undoubtedly been reassured by some attending family member that everything would be fine while I was away at the hospital. I do not think I have ever in my life fought tears as hard as I did then. I remember saying to him, "Well... baby, he's not." And he paused, looked at me, incredulously, and said, "Dad's DEAD?" The words themselves were a monstrous blow to my soul, but what caught me off guard, and sent my heart to emotional suicide watch, was the look on his *face*, as if he was living his deepest fear, his own personal nightmare. Instead of retching into the sink and crawling away to hide, by the grace of God, I managed to say very carefully, without spilling a tear, "No.... he had to go to heaven. But he is not coming back here. And you *will* see him one day, when you go to heaven, too. I promise." He nodded, hugged me, and did not say another word about it for a long time. My little warrior. I still replay that conversation in my head now, years later. It still amazes me that he never cried.

FUNERALS

When I was very small, I witnessed my first dead person. My uncle Gary had died suddenly and, naturally, my parents had brought little toddler me along to the wake. I remembered being hoisted up by my dad, so that I could see into the casket. My mind at that age, whether accurate or not, for some reason remembered his eyelids being sown shut with black thread. It scared me. I remember staring with no recognition of this person, and no real understanding of death, but I knew this person was not asleep. I did not want to look anymore. My parents say I was barely 2-years old, and could not possibly remember that. This vivid memory stays with me and since then I have opted out of funerals at every chance.

When I was 17, my grandfather died. He and I were close. He used to call me "so sweet" every time I visited. Going to his funeral was very hard, but I felt I should. My best friend came with me and I sat in the middle pew, off to the side of the church, keeping his body in the casket out of my line of sight. My cousin took our Granddad's death harder than anyone I had ever witnessed in real life; he displayed an inconsolable pain and loss of the only father figure he had, screaming and crying, trying to climb into the casket. His father was my uncle, the one whose funeral was my first. It was more than hard to watch. Again, I vowed to avoid funerals.

Jason's funeral was one thing I NEVER intended to be present for, let alone this soon. I wanted nothing to do with the preparation or purchases. I handed all of the burdens to his parents. Looking back on it, I suppose it was selfish and rather rude of me to not assume my wifely duties of burying my husband. At the time, I just wanted to sleep until I died and never have to face another day without him again. I refused to return to our home in Annapolis (and never would, in my mind) and my children and I moved in with my parents.

One day before the funeral, a few of my friends had taken me shopping, to get me out of the house and to buy something to wear to the funeral. I think I would have sooner put my own skin up for auction than look for a dress for this occasion, but I went, sullen and silent. We shopped for a black dress, a black "fancy widow hat," and accessories, because for some reason the tradition, as I was told, is that you look your best at your husband's funeral. Seemed to be a pretty stupid custom to me, but I obliged in my zombie state, only going through the motions. We found some nice things; the dress was especially nice and expensive. I took the things to the counter to pay for them and after searching deep into my purse I found that my wallet was missing.

As distressing as that was, the most curious thing happened then; amongst the things in my purse that were not what I was looking for, there was Jason's wallet, almost smiling at me. Now that I had reported him deceased, his credit cards should have been useless, but something told me to just try anyway. I told my friends my dilemma and reached into his wallet, pulling out a checking card from the bank account we shared. The cashier looked sympathetic, listening to my plight respectfully, not responding. Much to my surprise, she ran the card… and it worked! Tears welled up into my eyes as one of my girlfriends said exactly what I was thinking: "He bought you one more dress to wear." There is no way any of them could have known that the first thing Jason ever bought me had also been a dress I needed at the last minute. When we were in college and he asked me to be in a charity fashion show and I had replied that I had nothing to wear. We were only friends at the time, but he took me to Sears and bought me a beautiful black lace dress, no questions asked. Now that I think about it, I want to be buried with those two dresses. Hope someone remembers.

The actual funeral event remains a blur to me. I wore hot pink peep-toe heels with my black dress and black Sunday hat. If he was there in spirit I wanted him to see me looking good. It was, admittedly, a weird thought. Looking back I suppose underneath blankets of pain there was still me. I was in there somewhere, even if I could not speak it or show it…I knew I had not lost me completely. I had a desire to display the bright undying spirit within myself, to let everyone know I was not defeated. I would not lose myself amongst the depression nor would I surrender myself to mourning forever. I did not know how, but I would stand. I could be brave. I refused to just fade into black. It is kind of a silly notion that pink shoes could say all that. That little spark inside me however…it was all I had left. I was running on fumes.

I remember I could bring myself to do no more than sit outside the church and sob. I never wanted to see him in a coffin, in the ground, or the color of the coffin for that matter… so I just would not look. He and I had talked about it several times before in our random, sprawling conversations, and we had actually promised each other we would not go to each other's funerals, whoever died first. We had agreed it would be more than either of us could handle. Those memories and mental images we could both gladly do without.

People watched me sitting outside and sat near me while I struggled to stay sane, listening to the funeral speeches over an intercom. My aunt walked by to remind me to show dignity and to keep my chin up… but her husband was not dead; she did not understand. I lifted my chin and tried, but I could not focus on her sentiment. Someone sang a beautiful song; I thank God I cannot remember the name of it. I asked my brother to record the speeches and ceremony; he did better. He filmed it and from far enough away that should I ever decide to watch it, I still would not have to endure seeing my love in a casket. When I did finally watch it, almost two years later, I found that the speeches were clear and there were a lot of people that came to show their love for Jason. His fraternity brothers did some ritualistic pin thing where one of his favorite brothers had the honor of donating his own fraternity pin to Jason to be buried with. His mother wrote a beautiful poem that made me see her in a completely different light; one that reminds me now to hold my sons closer, kiss them more often, and baby them just a little longer. She had lost her baby.

Granted, she was able to see him grow and he had given her grandchildren, but he was her *first* baby! Little feet, little hands, little smiles—gone now, in a casket in the ground. As horrible as her pain must have been, I could process no more than what had already nailed my heart to the back of my throat. .

In the days and weeks that followed, I just wanted it all to be over. I literally remember feeling like every morning I was doing something wrong. Like if I did it right, imagined him there, imagined being in our bed, in our house, and reached out to touch him… I really could just open my eyes and this crazy, unrealistic nightmare would be over. Nightmare… such an accurate cliché.

The most hopeful (realistic) thought that I could muster was: "I can't wait until 5 years from now, when the pain is over, and I've moved on with my life." I wanted nothing more than to look back at this as just a memory. Distant. Over. Done.

I had a long way to go.

Two

PICKING UP THE PIECES

"I don't cry much at all, for a few good reasons. One of them is actually kind of funny. I hate crying because of how embarrassing it is for me; no matter what the occasion is, my nose turns bright red and becomes…let's use the words "excessively runny." More so than the average person's nose, I'm convinced. LOL. I always feared this one little scenario in my head where I'm in the heat of some romantic moment with some incredibly cute guy and tears of joy are perfectly appropriate, so I cry …and cue the 'nose waterfall' - TOTALLY ruining it - and that poor guy has no help to offer but his 'manly' shirt sleeves. It was pretty funny actually. The good news is when that moment did come, Jason never made fun of me about it. I just knew he'd always be there —and would hold me, runny nose and all.

The other reason I'd often hold the tears back, as if nothing were wrong at all, was fear. I seriously felt (and sometimes I still do) like if I gave into the real tears, the real pain, and the real tsunami of anger and sadness and disappointment – that I would lose my mind, my grip on reality, and my sense of control. I'd drown and burn and never come back to sanity if I gave in to those tears, or opened the floodgates to that kind of despair. I was scared to death... or by death, rather. Scared to lose control."[1]

Jason's death took me through many stages. After exhausting other avenues of coping with my pain—denial, silence, excessive sleeping, not eating, etc.—I wrote this blog and realized something interesting. I realized "losing control" was the thing that I was truly afraid of; it was my demon, the thing holding me hostage in my feelings of depression and defeat. I came to the epiphany that perhaps the root of the fear of loss is just that – the feeling of not being able to control certain things we have become accustomed to being part of our lives. Maybe the root of any fear really... is to not be able to control the outcome of a dire situation. I realized being able to pin point it, to name it, gave me the specific tool I needed to combat it. Try as I might, there was no escaping the fact that there was only one answer left. It gave me the solution I'd been running from the whole time because I wasn't sure I truly believed. I felt unworthy because of my doubts. Aren't true believers supposed to have unshakeable faith? But all I had left was God, for who is in control of everything? Who do the psalms and books and preachers say I can cast all fears to, He who controls all things, and has the end-all say in everything that happens?

It wasn't some miracle sermon or opening of the sky and angel songs that brought me to God. I was actually pretty angry with Him for everything I was going through and I had stopped speaking to him or going to church for quite some time. But during that while, even though I had my parents, friends, tons of support because people loved Jason, I felt completely alone. No one understood my specific pain. No one could say anything to comfort me. No one could answer my questions of what was next, how could I move on, and what would a life like mine be like now? In many ways, I felt like I was still sitting on the cold tile of that hospital floor. So, quite reluctantly, I went back to church.

---

1 An Entry from my blog, *CurlyMamaSwag,* on blogspot.com.

*"Train a child in the way he should go, and
when he is old he will not turn from it."*

~Proverbs 22:6

I had not been super religious in a long time. Jason and I were churchgoing people and he had recently been saved, giving his life to God. I had my own reservations. So I had my parents to thank, for though I was not living in the way that I should go, I had been trained in it. When it was time to return, I did.

I definitely did not transform into Sister Mary Clarence, sprout wings, or start running around churches during service or anything. I barely went back to church right away; I still am inconsistent at times, but there was a "quickening" so to speak, in my mind and soul. I needed God. I wanted the pain to be over, to just get back to being "normal," but more than that, I wanted the peace that people seemed to have when they had a real relationship with God. I could already see the tragedy to triumph story happening, I just couldn't figure out how to get there, how to move my story along, hurry up, and be at peace so that I too could have a happy, successful "But God!" ending.

I wanted to be someone else, something I had never been before. Someone new. My good friend gave me a book entitled, *When Everything Changes, Change Everything*, which encouraged a transformation of the mentality as a coping mechanism for dramatic change in one's life. What would my overall transformation look like? After regaining my faith, my next step was my career. I knew I wanted to be a writer, but with a degree in technology and a background of eight years doing so, finding a job at the bottom of the ladder in the writing field was not really going to cut it in the bills department. This single mommy person I had found myself struggling to be was working full-time with an upside down mortgage and two kids that ate like lumberjacks. At the time, one was an infant! Daycare, diapers, and *non-lactose* formula — oh my! I needed a plan; it lead me to brainstorm some more on what else I wanted to be. In my mind's eye, I knew what my dreams were and I pictured what I wanted to be.

I felt so helpless in my new state of being, so raw and exposed that I wanted to be able to arm myself, to fight back whatever came next. If pain, lack of finances, sickness, or parenting woes came at me and tried to knock me over like my husband's death did…I wanted to be ready the next time. I made a vow to never be caught off my guard and rolled by life like this again. I reinvented myself, taking the parts of who I wanted to be and fusing them together and placing them onto the blank slate I felt I was without my old life.,,, tweaking them until it was totally me, Me 2.0.

Lastly, I had to decide if I wanted to move on from my marriage and try to accept a new person into my life. I had to face being a single mother, dating (Dun-dun-dun- dun-DUN). I had to pack up my suitcase of "wishing I was cooler" and my two children and get on the road to single parent dating eventually. I know, most people would say to wait… love will come… yada, yada, yada. And all that is true; however, it is also true that the easiest way to move the heart is with distraction and sometimes taking that road is better than doing donuts on memory lane. It was definitely not all freedom and soggy romance novels, to say the least. It was hard. It still is. But I learned many… many … MANY lessons, simply in HOW to move forward from a substantial set back… from ANY setback, and I believe my path to personal development involves sharing what I learned and maybe helping someone else!

Six years later, I can now say I am definitely not the same woman I was when my husband passed away. I am stronger, more confident, more independent, and better equipped to raise my children than I ever was before. I still have a lot of room to grow, but I learned so much about myself along the way. I am happy to say that even though I will never stop feeling the pain of loss, I can stand and say yes, there IS an "other side" of grief and depression and I have finally come out on that other side.

Three

Yes, It Happened to YOU

*Y*es, YOU. I think the hardest thing to accept, when it comes to drastic, life-changing events is the fact that it happened to you. At least, that is what it was for me. My worst fears, the worst-case scenario, the ultimate loss or setback, were always lurking around in the back of my mind. I normally dismissed them as paranoia or waved them away over a good girl talk session, calling it my "overactive imagination." It did not make them go away; the gloom-and-doom thoughts would still interrogate my brain with "what-ifs" in the wee hours of the longest nights. But then, I still did not expect them to actually happen. Sometimes though, (obviously) the worst actually DOES happen. That one thing that you just knew you would never recover from or never imagined yourself actually living through – becomes your new reality. Just like that – BAM! You have a whole new life to figure out now.

Interestingly, despite all your worrying and prepping for the worst in your imagination, you are still blindsided when it hits. You keep trying to wake up, you keep questioning whether it is real, and you cannot understand how everyone else is accepting this thing! You want to shake people by the shoulders and refuse to participate in this altered reality. You may even withdraw from the outside world, holing up in your room, and simply hold in any reaction until you are sure this is YOUR life and YOUR body you currently inhabit.

You want to kick and scream and demand answers from whomever you believe has the power to answer the questions: WHY is this happening, WHERE is my old life, and WHAT did I do to deserve this?

So yeah, I get that. I went through it and unfortunately, this is normal. You are one of millions of people before you, and millions after you, that will experience at least *once*, while on this planet, an event that either:

A. Makes you a stronger individual
B. Breaks the very fabric of your sanity, or
C. Both

Does the fact that most people will at some point go through some life changing experience diminish the severity or validity of that individual's feelings toward it or as a result of it? Hell, no. You have a right to feel these things. You also have a right to do whatever it takes (within the confines of the law!) to bounce back. I wrote this book to declare to you, the griever, the one who has lost something - not only do you have the right to feel these things, but as long as you have breath in your body, you own the CHOICE to *repair* yourself, repurpose your life, move on, and to even be *happy* again. Yes, you have the option to win, even after enduring a *great* loss.

For me, the choice was to:

Stay on the hospital floor, never mentally recover, and forfeit my independence, and give up my children.

-OR-

Get up, figure it out, and face being a 28-year-old widow and mom.

I could have left my sanity in the waiting room when I was told my handsome, vegetarian, wonderful husband had died of a random head injury while *playing* with our children on EASTER DAGGONE SUNDAY (Yeah, I was pretty upset with God about that at the time. I probably *still* harbor some feelings about it)! Nobody would have blamed me at all for losing my mind right then and maybe never getting it back! But, I did not. I was not a warrior, I was not strong, I was not born with some superpower that made me any better than anyone else. I made a choice. I will not lie to you and say it is an easy, push button, Nike-Just-Do-It choice, but I promise you, it IS your choice. I wrote this book to map out what to do once you've made that choice—the choice that gets you through your storm, no matter how big your storm is. Ready?

Good, Let's Get Started!

I am not going to bore you with the different phases of grief. I will say, yes, they are real and relevant. You may not go through all of them or in the order you will find in the support group brochures, but more than likely…some of the feelings of loss will come into play. What I will also point out is that feelings resulting from being in a state of grief, apply to MANY situations. Grief is just what we feel when we lose things. "Loss" is what they should call it instead, since it seems more accurate. What types of loss am I talking about? You want to make sure this book is for you? Dealing with grief and loss comes with the package when losing ANY of the following:

- Job/Career
- Health due to Drug Abuse/Dependency
- Loved ones (death)
- Sense of Purpose/ Loss of Belief System
- Divorce
- Failed Business
- Self Confidence
- Home Foreclosure
- Posttraumatic Stress
- Money/Bad Credit/Bankruptcy
- Mobility (Illness/Amputation)
- Friendship/Relationship breakups
- Disability
- Life threatening Illnesses

The list goes on and on!

There are specific phases of "grief" in plenty of books that most people can relate to going through at some point in time. I will probably mention some of them as we get further into this book, but one thing I will not do is "diagnose" you to pieces. I do not believe in giving people "clinical" reasons to behave irrationally, have pity parties, or self-medicate due to a new "condition" they have been sold by the latest Doctor Oz episode. No offense to old Ozzie, he has one of the better quality self-improvement TV shows; I just do not believe everything can be cured with raw coconut oil or yoga or the newest butt-shaper contraption on the market now. Sometimes people *need* to hear the truth that, yes, overcoming loss will take time and you cannot expect that 'fixing' something external is going to heal something internal. Loss is internal; overcoming it is an internal journey. My situation, in my opinion, was extreme and put me in both mental and physical despair. Not everyone will go through such extreme situations, but mental and physical health are so vital to everyday life, they don't have to endure extreme damage to still need repair. If you have ever found yourself in a situation such as anxiety disorder, depression, eating disorders, or even low self-esteem, you already know these are conditions that need to be addressed as soon as possible.

Six years later, I still have anxiety disorder, I am still a single parent, and I still miss my husband very much. So no, I am not going to tell you that getting fit, eating better, or taking some anti-depression pill is the answer. The difference between now and then however, is I am healthy and very happy, and I can manage my anxiety, my children, and the occasional sad periods a WHOLE lot better with my mental and physical health back in control and a plan in place for obstacles that threaten my happiness and wellbeing.

What I offer in this book is the mental game plan I used to overcome my tragedy from the inside out. Fair enough? The first step of that game plan begins with the core of you—your faith.

CORE BELIEFS

I was never a Bible reader. I grew up Catholic and, I am sure, I knew the Apostle's Creed at some point, but never did I seem to find the time to really read the stories in the Bible. I knew about David and Goliath, Noah and his ark, and…that was about it. Something I noticed when I got older, among my friends of other denominations that went to church faithfully, was that they knew their Bibles! It unnerved me to no end that they could pull a Scripture at any given time, about any given situation – and once I heard the "life application" of this scripture, I would think – dang! Why don't I know THAT Bible story? They had peace because proof was within the Bible that things were temporary, things were all working for the glory of the Lord, and that everything was according to plan. I wanted that kind of peace. Badly.

When Jason died, I wanted nothing more than to just get back to being "normal." I wanted it to be OVER. I was finally sick of moping, sick of being depressed, and just plain sick and tired of being…cue the chorus… "Sick and Tired!" I wanted the peace that people seemed to have when they had a relationship with God. I could already see the tragedy and triumph story happening, I just could get there.

How? How? How? I wanted to know HOW to move my story along … so that I, too could have a happy, successful, "But God!" ending. Fortunately for me, God was listening. He put it on my heart that in order to have a God-ending, you have to start with God in your beginning, no matter how many times you have to begin.

Now, if you do not believe in God and Jesus Christ as your Lord and Savior—that does not disqualify you from getting what you need from this book. You can believe whatever you want to; I'm not here to judge you. As a Christian, I don't believe that's *my* job. In my religion, we have someone for that already! ☺ I will say, however that my God is a GOOD God, you can try Him and see – and if you do, tell Him I sent you for a sample!! Ha!

Whatever you believe in, be sure to thoroughly define your core beliefs because that is your sanity. A core belief is an unshakeable truth that no matter what happens to you, you can hold this to be true. Mine is built on this story.

THE RING OF PEACE

There was an eastern king who was very wealthy, but very unhappy. He had everything money could buy, but the happiness those possessions brought him was fleeting at best. One night, he had a dream in which he saw a beautiful gold ring. The next day, he called together his top advisors and wisest men and he said, "That ring in my dream will bring me happiness. I must have it, and you must go out into the world and find it for me."

Well, the king's advisors searched far and wide, and eventually found a ring whose quality and beauty was unparalleled, and so they bought it at a great price, and brought it to the king. The king was elated, and before he put the ring on his finger, he noticed an inscription on the inside that said, "This too shall pass."

And finally, the king realized that all the things he had sought for his happiness would pass away, including this great ring, and that as long as he placed his happiness and security in physical things, he might experience temporary happiness, but would never know lasting joy. That day he stopped chasing after temporary pleasures, and so the ring not only brought him the happiness he sought, but the joy he needed.

The message of this story reminds me that just as happy times cannot always last, sad ones cannot last forever either. Isn't that something? Christianity is designed to help us place our trust in God rather than the temporary things of this world. In our Scripture, we are reminded over and over again that all things shall, in due time, pass from existence. All things, that is, except God's love and his presence; they endure forever.

Once I established my core belief, I began to put it to work. Whenever I felt doubt or fear along the road of my transformation, I would apply it. I could say to myself, *what was the last thing I felt doubtful about? What did I do? Looking back, was it really worth all of my worrying?*

Regardless of what the result was, applying my core belief, "This too shall pass," I was able to realize that doubt and fear are a waste of time. I made whatever decision I felt was best at the time, realizing the fears and doubts I had about the results were usually unnecessary. If I made a mistake, it was a lesson; if I made the correct choice, it was a direct result of a previous lesson. Either way, it endured for the time it was meant to and then it was over.

 ### Scratch Pad

*Throughout the book, when you see the "Scratch Pad", it means we are going to take a little break from reading to participate in an activity that will APPLY the topics of discussion to **your** life, to help you understand the process of **your** personal recovery. Feel free to write in the book, or break out your own pen and pad if you need more space. Ready? Let's get you on the road to moving forward!*

Writing down your obstacles and finding resolutions visually is an important tool in your recovery. Try to answer these questions with as much detail as possible.

What is <u>one</u> of your most current, relevant obstacles?

_____

_____

When was the last time you had an obstacle or knew someone who had a similar one?

_____

_____

_____

_____

_____

Looking back on that obstacle, was that obstacle as bad as you thought it was? Do you think it would have been easier if you had known you would be all right?

_____

_____

_____

_____

_____

Now, push it further.

If you could be certain that, just like last time, you would get through this new obstacle… if you knew without a shadow of a doubt, that you would win, in some shape or form... how differently would you go about this current obstacle? This is how I used my faith as my confidence. All the time, people say, "Have Faith" or "Stand on God's word. Step out on Faith," but they never really explain HOW. My definition of how to *use* faith is using past triumphs from my past problems to fuel what I call my "now peace", or my peaceful outlook on any current problem.

Past problem + Past triumph = Fuel for "Now Peace".

When you can use your faith at will, I learned, you could make this your confidence. I gathered more verses for my arsenal because not all of my trials that I faced during my growth process could be consoled by one passage. Sometimes that inner voice that worries when I know better, that keeps me up at night when I need to rest, introducing fear and doubt where confidence should be – would need more convincing. I learned to use doxologies (a liturgical formula of praise to God) like "Now unto Him!" which is a short phrase that calls the Scripture of Jude 1:24:

"Now unto him who is able to keep you from falling and to present you before his glorious presence without fault and with great joy."

And another favorite that sounds just like that one is Ephesians 3:20:

"Now unto him that is able to do exceeding abundantly above all that we ask or think, according to the power that works in us..."

Long story short, my inner peace began with my faith and came from creating a safe house for my soul and mind. In my safe house, I kept my core beliefs, my triumphs, my restored confidence, my sense of logical reassurance, and my doxologies, for that extra boost the word of God gave me.

Four

ACCEPTANCE

Accepting Yourself

Among the many seemingly unproductive things I did in the wake of my loss—sleep, eat, retreat to my room to be alone—the first thing I *needed* to do was to accept my process. I was very strongly against participating in grief support processes involving steps, therapy, medication for depression, and other conventional "cures" for life's curve balls, and generally being told that something was wrong with ME. The only thing, in fact, that was wrong with me was my thinking about my position. What I wish I had done sooner was to accept what had happened so that I could assess my damages and from there, move forward with a new plan of action. First and foremost, I needed to realize I was going to need TIME and PATIENCE.

Everyone has his or her own healing time. Do not waste energy feeling guilty about the time it is taking you to snap back! Take it, live it, and when you get sick and tired of it – that is how you know it is time to take another step forward! In my time of healing, I did quite a bit of what I called 'coddling and coping'. I basically did whatever felt good at the time. I was as gentle with myself as possible; I cried when I wanted to, I slept when I wanted, I spent time with my children when I was at my best, and I arranged for family to care for them when I was not.

The Hard Facts

While you are getting your mind settled about the fact that this will not be an overnight recovery, when you are ready, the next thing to do is to try your best to accept and deal with the hard facts. The hard facts are just that: hard. I read somewhere in a book for grief support, that I literally needed to hear them, aloud, in order to really face them as reality. According to the book it was "healthy" to speak the truth of a loss aloud to oneself, daily, constructing a mantra stating the negative and the positive sides of the truth, and then a positive affirmation, or action you will make as a result of it.

I felt ridiculous, speaking aloud in the mirror every morning, it took me weeks to actually start doing it; and honestly nothing seemed to change, not the first day or the fifth. But sometime after that, eventually, I would catch myself in the mirror while I repeated the mantra of the day, smiling…. just a little. Not really about the facts I was stating; more so about the fact that I had set a goal, stuck to it, and I was on my way.

My mantra went something like this:

> *It is not a dream. I don't have a time machine. There is nothing I can do or could have done to change things. I accept that. They are what they are and I can only move forward, not back. My life will be different now. What I DO about these changes now is more important than the change itself. I have the ball now.*

The best part about that last statement though is that even though the changes in my life had taken control for a moment, the worst of the storm was over. It happened, but now I was back in control. It was my turn to move, ball in my court. After I could wrap my mind totally around that, I picked up a few affirmations to combat the negative feelings I encountered due to some of the facts I was facing.

Affirmations are short, powerful statements that not only give life to truths that have yet to come into being, but they also give reassurance and confidence to the speaker. They have to mean something to YOU. I have found they help tremendously if used in daily repetition. I know you have heard it before, that your "words become your actions and your thoughts become your truths"? Or perhaps "the power of life and death lies in the tongue?" Could not be truer. Why do you think people use and reuse the same quotes over and over? They are usually a unique string of words woven together to motivate a specific thought or action. Some people pass them off as clever or witty clichés – but I see them as powerful.

Here are some affirmations that I needed at this time and that might help you where you are now:

- I am hurt, but I am OK.
- No one needs me to do anything but my best.
- It doesn't matter whose fault it is; blaming people never fixed anything.
- I will need time to heal.
- It is a process and I WILL COME OUT when I am ready.
- I will bounce back!
- It has happened to other people and even though that doesn't mean much to me now, at least I KNOW I am not alone.
- If I want to, I can talk to other people. When I'm ready.
- My life is NOT over, it's just DIFFERENT.
- The change is in MY hands now. I decide what's next with my actions.

Jim Rohn, a very successful motivational speaker, author, and businessman (and also one of my personal favorites) said: "Affirmation without discipline is the beginning of delusion." Have you ever said something to yourself, made a goal, or had an idea that you were 100% committed to until the next week came around? Maybe the next few days you were already over it, had already decided that goal was too lofty or poorly planned? Affirmations are reassurances of truths that can only come to pass if discipline is applied. Discipline is hard for everyone, or else it would have come in a little bag in your little baby hand at birth. You have to work at it. Some have to work harder than others (like me because I have a lazy streak!), but the work is required nonetheless. The way I disciplined myself with my affirmations was to use three simple rules:

1. Post affirmations someplace VISIBLE and read them every day.
2. Decide what small, routine ACTIONS can be taken each day to prove this affirmation true (Example: daily goal setting).
3. Do NOT start over. Do not quit because you skipped a day, or two, or fifteen. Stop expecting to be perfect and just pick up where you left off.

Accepting Help

Ok, this is a big one. Big, fat, hairy and huge. *No one* likes to be told they cannot do something on their own or to admit they need help. This vehement defending of one's capability to independently cope with what is going on around them is very normal. Having two children, I would estimate it starts sometime around being a toddler, probably two years old – and you grow up, but it never really lets you go! That "I can do it MYSELF! NO! NO! NO!" Feeling when someone treats you like you are fragile because of your loss can be pretty hard to keep inside.

Important things like running a business, caring for children, balancing a career, and just carving out time to tend to your OWN needs can all become huge stressors because they demand *day to day* attention. They do not usually allow for unplanned emotional break-downs or healing time, and trust me, you need breaks! What you do not need is the *physical* harm and *emotional* stress that *not* taking time outs and *not* acknowledging your own needs can inflict on your body and mind. If only to provide these breaks, you really may need just a little help, with some things that can be attended to while you take care of yourself.

My biggest pet peeve, when my husband passed, was for my mother to come in to my house with her own key and start "helping me clean". As if grieving, working full time, and taking care of a two children was not enough, I felt like she expected my house to be spotless! And then she would move things, and I'd never be able to find it – it was so frustrating! To me, that was the *worst* thing she could do! But to her, it was just the opposite. She figured that was the *best* thing she could do, because she knew I was grieving and trying to juggle my new, very busy life. She thought a clean house would help me feel better. That was her way of showing she cared. People who want to help you are not mind readers. As inconvenient and annoying as that is, you have to meet people where they are.

I've found that the best way to tolerate accepting help with my everyday needs was controlling the WAY in which I allowed someone to help. Overstepped boundaries and insensitivities to your needs can be avoided by simply knowing what you need and being able to articulate exactly how much help (or how little!) you want. I swear things were so much easier when I realized *how* I wanted to be helped, and no longer had to be frustrated that I needed it. You take a person's willingness to help you and then *you* take control of *how*. Thank them, tell them, "I love you, Person-who-loves-me-while-I'm-going-through-Hell," and let them help! You just tweak whatever they are willing to do so that it does not annoy the crap out of you! For example:

<u>Scratch Pad</u>

Here we are again, at the scratch pad. This time, let's make two lists:

Stuff I do not mind WHEN it gets done or WHO does it.

-
-
-
-
-
-

Stuff I'll FREAK OUT if people do without asking.

-
-
-
-
-
-

After the anxiety attacks, weight battles, and sleep deprivation… I learned the really hard way. I do not recommend taking that class[2] at ALL. Nonetheless, I learned that eventually, as much as you would rather not, you have to let people in to help you in the ways that you are falling behind due to your healing time. That brings me to the last part of acceptance in a time of loss:

Accept that all therapy is Not "Crazy" Therapy

If you could just roll your eyes as loudly as possible, right here, you would be me, at the slightest mention of therapy, therapeutic activities, or anything close to it. When you lose something devastating, like a spouse or job, and people expect you to go a little off the deep end – it can feel insulting. It made me want to scream: I am NOT CRAZY! I'm not fragile! I am just sad and trying to move on!

I get it. I know how it feels to strongly dislike the idea of therapy and the assumptions about people that need it. I also never understood how someone or something *outside* my head could possibly help *me* with what is going on *inside* my head – so that I can fix the things that *I* did not break! I did not cause this loss, so why do I have to fix ME and MY life because of it? And furthermore, any weakness I had in my own head is my business and my problem to solve. End of discussion! Humph! ß that was usually my reply when asked about therapy: ranting and asking circular questions, probably sounding like a perfect impression of my father (Love you, Daddy).

Unfortunately, I was going to find the answer to exactly why I needed therapy. I tried ignoring the grief. I just did not deal with it at all. I would not talk about it, I went back to my job, friends, and parenting as best as I could, surrounded myself around other people whose lives were fine while mine felt

---

2 "Don't Take that Class" – from Jim Rohn's *How to Win Friends and Influence People or, The Law of Sowing and Reaping* (Excerpt from "Building Your Network Marketing Business" single CD). It basically means do not worry too much about the "why" of that specific matter. Do not study it – it is not worth finding out first hand. Take the advice and run.

in shambles. Sometimes I would listen to random 'motivational speeches' from friends and family who were convinced they could "talk" to me and compare their losses on an equal playing field, (not that their pains were lesser, I just could not relate) when they had no idea what I was going through; that actually bothered me more than not talking at all. Ignoring the feelings and phases I needed to go through and express made me feel explosive, overly sensitive, and even more isolated. I felt like they were treating me differently because of my loss, and that left me feeling misunderstood and alone. So I don't recommend that at all. That sucked.

Eventually, I tolerated conversations with my mother about 'going to the stupid therapy'. I was not interested in group therapy, or talking with other people who had gone through similar situations because that just seemed counterproductive. Who wants to cry in a room with people who are also crying? I'd just feel like a multi-headed sack of helplessness, then! I learned I was very wrong about this kind of therapy, group sessions can be extremely productive and supportive. In time, I would be introduced to someone who had gone through the exact same loss as me – and to this day I have never connected with anyone else the way I have with that friend. People are out there who have shared the same specific pain and grief that you have and giving them a chance to share your burden with you, share their remedies and coping mechanisms, and listen when no one else understands…is truly priceless. Early on in my process, however, I had decided not to be open to it.

You may need therapy, and may need more --or less than I did. What I needed was a full assessment of my situation and a clear game plan of who I am, who I wanted to be, and how to get there from my present state. It was uncomfortable to start the process, but did I die, endure being treated like 'a crazy' or have to take mind altering medicine like I'd been so afraid seeing a 'shrink' would lead to? Nah. It wasn't terrible at all. In fact, I owe much of my progress and positive outlook to that wonderful lady, my psychologist, the late Dr. Susan Bernstein.

Part 11 – Assess

Five

ASSESSING YOUR SITUATION

*F*reedom and happiness are best found with the ease of which one moves through change. In other words, the better you receive the changes in your life, the easier it is to be happier, and to be free from worry, stress, and craziness that change can potentially bring. It is definitely easier said than done, but what is helpful is to learn with any difficult change in your life, is this: Instead of giving away your control, and allowing the change to wreck your mood, day, situation, or even your life, make accurate assessments of the situation. From there you can take control, and formulate the best plan on how to react.

For example: If there is a baseball speeding toward your face and you could freeze time, step back and take a "bigger picture" assessment of your current, accurate situation, you would think: *Do I have time to move out of the*

way, cover my face, or possibly catch it? Is it a hard ball or a soft ball? Could I maybe stop it or change its direction?

Phase One: The Total Assessment

Assessing the whole situation allows you to move with the change and react sensibly, with less drama, and possibly avoid some excessive pain. If you had done nothing, screamed and stood there, frozen by your perception of what the situation looks like instead of focusing on what you could DO about it, then nothing is accomplished but the ball smacking you in the face…and probably a great deal of pain. The great thing about change is it's not a baseball speeding toward your face. Change may happen just as quickly, but you have the capability to decide at *any point in time* how to react. You have the mental capability at any point to take an accurate assessment of the whole situation, and change your trajectory with the decisions you make thereafter. When you step back and get a clear picture of what is really going on – not focusing on the emotions resulting from what it looks like, you can regain control: moving *through* changes in life, instead of having them move you.

After having my first son, who was a little over 10 pounds at birth, (yeah…big baby for a little lady!) I felt like I had been unjustly plucked from my life long category of "super healthy athlete" and dropped off into the "out-of-shape, depressed mom" box. I had stretch marks on my everything and my skin had completely ignored the lotions and creams I had slathered on for 10 months prior. My stomach was a road map to Disasterland and from the caesarian section operation needed to deliver such a large baby and the doctors had called the damage "irreparable without a tummy tuck". I was almost 30 pounds heavier than before I got pregnant. My second 10-pound child came five years later and, though I thought I was busy loving my children more than anything, shortly after having him I was diagnosed with post-partum depression. I worked from home, so I was alone, tethered to relentless, back-to-back calls from my help desk headset, sobbing uncontrollably, and barely eating within the 8-9 hour daily stretch …and this went on for about a year. The irony is I was working the help desk when *I was the one* who needed help!

My husband did everything he could to help me around the house, taking on the daily activities with both of the kids, but I saw the toll it was taking on him. He was beginning to feel the weight of my not being able to help out. He grew slightly distant, running on autopilot around the house while I slept, getting up early and disappearing with the boys to "give mommy her peace." We did not talk as much and our "perfect" relationship became pretty tense at times. Toward the end of that year, I was being hospitalized every weekend it seemed. I was having severe anxiety attacks and needed testing for possibly hidden autoimmune diseases like Celiac or Lupus. Jason became even more distant, unable to relate to my sadness and inexplicable pains, even though he had been through depression before. He grew frustrated with the helplessness he felt because he could not fix me. As I worsened, I was angry with myself because I was not "snapping back," I was not getting better.

When I thought nothing could get worse, early that next year was when Jason died. But that part of the story you know. What few people really knew was, on top of that, my job, three months after, laid me off *over the phone*. My mortgage was completely impossible without two incomes and the bank that held my mortgage informed me that I made too much money as an unemployed widow for them to lower the payments. They also let me know that I would have to default (begin to be late or stop paying) on my home loans to get any help from them. Talk about being kicked when you are down!

Mentally and emotionally, those events were what it took to break me. I was completely shattered. I felt like I had nothing, like a returned mail-order bride. I had to start completely over, back at my parents' house – this time, with kids.

The Doctor Is In

My first mistake, with all those issues tumbling down over me, was thinking all these negatives made up my *total situation*. This chapter is about properly assessing the total situation.

When you are sad or feeling defeated for long enough, it becomes physical. Depression is almost like being sick—you begin to feel tired, have sudden aches and pains, allergies may worsen, preexisting conditions like migraines could be compounded; it is like you have a long-term flu. You may feel like you cannot do anything and everything sucks. You may have thoughts like "if _____ hadn't happened," or "if _____ wasn't my current situation," you would be able to focus more on your daily missions, get more done, and generally have a much better quality of life. Even though that is not necessarily true, nothing can really hinder you if you can be creative enough to think your way around it; still, you may have a tough time figuring out **where to start.**

When being sad and anxious begins to have a physical affect, that physical affect tends to become the biggest factor of lack of motivational change. So that is where I decided to start my total assessment: physical health.

Physical Assessment

I hate the doctor's office. I hate the smell. I hate the colors and I hate the sick people. Hate. Hate. Hate. In some cases, it is accurate to say I would rather eat a whole box of hair than go to the doctor.

However, (in my medical disclaimer voice) sometimes depression or feelings of loss can manifest themselves in physical ways and it is important to rule out any physical issues there might be. Emotional loss can lead to lack of sleep, eating disorders, and a whole slew of outside dependencies and coping mechanisms that could put your health at risk. Getting a professional to evaluate your status can give you the tools to fix whatever is going on physically and also boost your morale emotionally once you realize that the aches, pains, and lack of energy were normal and totally not as serious as you may have thought they were. I needed to step back and see the whole picture if I was going to do something about it.

So, with my weight climbing and my depression worsening with each anxiety attack and the stress of raising kids in my parents' house, I began to realize there was no other way to fight back – I was going to have to start from somewhere. Was I sick? Did I have some rare deadly disease or maybe per-manent mental damage from my circumstances? Not knowing and worrying about that would cause an anxiety attack alone! So I plucked up all my courage and went to the dumb old appointment.

I was nervous, sweating, and needed a bag to breathe in by the time my name was finally called in the waiting room. I had imagined all kinds of things were wrong. My faith in myself was broken and I figured life would just keep throwing me lemons. By the grace of God, the doctor had not turned out to be a new lemon. Physically – I was fine. Technically, I was not even over-weight, just out of shape and needed more sleep. The shock for me was that this meant it was ALL IN MY HEAD. *So I am crazy now,* I thought. *Awesome.* In hindsight, the trip had actually given me what I needed: an assessment, a picture of what I was really working with and a place to start my journey of healing.

Mental Assessment

Since I had adamantly ruled out any and all other suggestions of grief therapy, the only thing left to do was to go to a one-on-one psychiatrist, for the anxiety. After VERY reluctantly agreeing with my mother to ONLY see a psychologist/therapist once a week, with my oldest son --for him, not me -- my ideas about that began to slowly change, too. Dr. Bernstein was warm, practi-cal, and had decided to counsel both Justin and I, for whatever we needed. Justin enjoyed his individual session and, over time, made the healthy adjust-ment to the loss of his dad. After a few visits I began looking forward to seeing her. I liked her personality, and slowly I was beginning to think differently about the whole idea of having a 'shrink'.

Turns out I was not crazy either (thanks again, Jesus). What I took from those visits was that the best treatment for mental issues like depression, grief, or anxiety, was allowing someone with better mental organizational skills and tools to coach me through the process of moving forward from tragedy. As a matter of fact, it became clear to me that the cure for my mental issues was not going to be a quick fix like pills or hypnosis (I tried them both). I found my help in talking to someone who could coach me through the uncertainties of moving on and moving forward from tragedy. I wouldn't need to go for years either; in fact I only had about twenty visits in all. What Dr. Bernstein did for me was simple. She just gave me a place to move forward *from*. Once I was sure of what I was working with, mentally and physically, it was time to begin the phases of moving forward. In the following appointments, and along the way on my own time, that is what I learned. It is important, getting from A to B, to know first where A is. In order to do that, we had to first look at where I had come from.

Phase Two: Past Assessment

My old self, the 'Maya' before my tragedies, was not exactly what I thought I would be at 30-years old. I was out of shape, not really acting on any of my dreams, and my life definitely was not very exciting. I loved my life, do not get me wrong, my husband was in it with me. I had him to swap "Sparta in the workplace" stories with, since we'd both hated our jobs at the time. I had him as my best friend to tag team with the two messiest, cutest kids in the world that we had made together. I loved being part of our little family, but... as an individual, I was doing nothing to enhance the experience of just being Maya. I had started a book, written a few poems, won a few contests online, but I was for the most part, all about my family. And that was fine with me. When I lost him, I felt I lost the centerpiece and glue to the family – I lost my identity. I felt homeless, nameless, and pointless. Yes, I was still me; I still had my kids, but I just felt like I was existing alongside them now, not really part of the action anymore. There was nothing and no one that was *just* for me. That's something I wish I'd told him; that I'd felt he was the only one on Earth that was, before we had the kids, here just for me.

Inside my head, I kept going over and over what I had lost. I was unable to grasp the hard fact that all that I was, all I had, and my life as I had known it before would only be memories from then on... and that I was helpless. I could not get it back, not without bringing back that exact situation. Everything now would be a substitute or replacement; anything close would just be a replica and a reminder of what was permanently gone.

When my therapist asked me to really detail my losses, it felt redundant. This soap opera was the only channel working in my head anyway, 24/7. On the contrary, when I talked about it and wrote it out with Dr. Bernstein, it was kind of validating. Having a chance to really see it on paper, it really felt good to acknowledge those feelings --somewhere else besides in my head-- and to get them out. It was still emotional, but it felt like proof I had a reason to be where I was, that just because I'd lost so much, I didn't have to feel like a loser. It felt less like a pity party and more like a starting block, a tangible place to put the things I wanted to push off from, and leave behind.

It also highlighted something that I had not given much thought to while in my depressed state of loss: I *still had* quite a few of the things that I described myself having before my losses. In my head, I felt I had lost everything, but in the visible inventory (which we are about to do next and hopefully, you will notice the same things I did), you realize: You never lose everything. Even if it feels that way. Some things cannot be taken away. So let's put those things down:

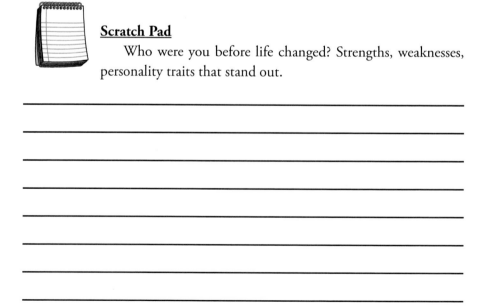

Scratch Pad
Who were you before life changed? Strengths, weaknesses, personality traits that stand out.

_____

_____

_____

_____

_____

_____

_____

_____

_____

_____

_____

What three things did you like about you, before your loss? What made you happy?

_____

_____

_____

_____

_____

_____

_____

_____

_____

_____

_____

_____

_____

What was GOOD and irreplaceable about your OLD situation?

_____

_____

_____

_____

_____

_____

_____

_____

_____

_____

_____

_____

What, after your loss, has stayed the same? What do you still have?

_____

_____

_____

_____

_____

_____

_____

_____

_____

Got you thinking? I hope so. At first some of these questions made me sad, more depressed, and seemed unnecessarily focused on the negative part of my predicament. I did not want to think about what I had or what I could not replace. However, talking about the things I did have left, or in spite of the loss of my husband made me feel stronger, and less alone.

What I learned is the point of assessment is to figure out where you want to go, what you're bringing with you, and what you're leaving behind. How can you do that without knowing where you came from, using what you've learned from back then, and building from there? You need to have lived in a house or at least been inside one previously to know how to build a new one. You have to know what it needs, what to fill it with, and how to take care of it. No use in scrapping that good knowledge just because the old house is gone. Use it. Gather it. Analyze it. Take with you what you can use to propel you forward, and leave the parts you don't need behind.

Six

WHO ARE YOU NOW? PRESENT ASSESSMENT

*N*ow that you have had a chance to get that out and look at whom you WERE and what you HAD on paper, let's do the next exercise.

"You are in a stage of 'being' right now, in your current situation, despite who you were and who you want to be. So let's describe what you are right now, like a character in one of your stories. Let's see what we are working with. Are you the 'independent single mom writer who likes her freedom and travels and lives life looking for adventure', or the 'tech girl next door that just wants a new best friend,'? Or maybe you're 'the hopeless romantic chick that just wants to hurry up and be in love and have a family again', or 'the football mom who spends all her time with her kids and is only looking for a father them'? You can be anything you want to be in the future, and change whatever you want – but who are you now?"

When my therapist, Susan, said this to me, I thought about it long and hard... I let it sink in. I thought about how there was a piece of me in each of those descriptions. I knew what I would wish to be if I had a magic wand... but who am I right now, in the wake of my tragedy? Who are YOU right now? What tools do you have to work with to get to where you want to be?

This takes a little more thought than you may have first assumed. Automatically, you begin to think of what the loss has forced you to become. We have already talked about what you had and had to leave behind. So now we can assess who you are and what you have right now as a result of that. At first, you will probably only come up with the negatives, but they are also part of the whole picture, so let's get those out of the way first. How has this loss impacted your everyday life? Your schedule? Think about how you feel physically—has anything changed? Is there time you have now that you used to spend doing something that you cannot anymore? Has your personal presentation, meaning how you present yourself (hygiene, attention to personal details, mood, clothing, or overall appearance) slackened? What about spiritually? Has your faith suffered?

Now, let's focus on the good things. Do not worry; you will get to write all of the other things down in just a second. I will put some trigger words in each writing area, so no worries about forgetting that train of thought! ADHD and OCD remember? I have totally got you covered!

What is good about your situation right now? What worked out or fell into place? What parts of your schedule are open now for something new? Did anything good stay the same? What positive people are in your life that you can turn to for support?

To allow you to see some possibly hidden blessings for yourself, I am going to use a basic Venn diagram to show how this exercise of taking inventory really works. It is like being lost in a forest, on foot, losing daylight; you need to know what you have working for you and against you and then use those facts to create a plan of how you will survive the night. Do you have food? A flashlight? Are you injured? Is there shelter? When you lay out what you have and put it against what you do not, it helps you see more clearly and focus on what you CAN DO to move forward

Phase Three: Present Assessment

Scratch Pad

On the next page, using short phrases or words, describe the changes or results of your loss or setback, the positives and negatives of your loss. I have suggested some key words below to help trigger some of your thoughts.

Oh, yeah, don't forget to turn the book sideways. ☺

Financial Other Dependencies
Meds Discoveries
Losses Lessons people Increased
documentation Learned life lose Freedom
Mood New Paperwork
Family Faith Sanity home Time
money Support Resume Decreased
Slate Personal
Schedule Gain Physical
Wills/Testament Responsibilities Clean
Changes Appearance Work
Updating

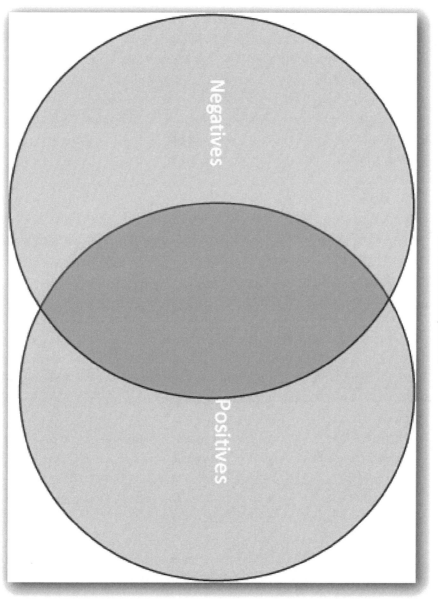

Because Of My Loss:

Negatives

Positives

Once you have both the positive and negative sides filled out, what do you do about that overlapping space in the middle? That is where, using both the negatives and the positives, you can brainstorm what options you have when you put them together. Using our woods example again, if your negative was that you were lost, and had broken your compass, and your positives were that you remembered from scouts class that moss grows mostly on the north side of trees in the northern hemisphere, putting those two together you could figure out which way the rest of the directions were! And hopefully, no longer be lost. If you were me, however… I'm going to hope you packed a charged cell phone. I haven't been a girl scout for a loooong time. ☺

Your focus must shift to in order to move forward. This is how you are going to begin your plans for right now, in the present, and the springboard for what you will plan for the near future! But, right now, let's not get ahead of ourselves; still let's focusing on the present: What possibilities and opportunities do you have NOW because of what you lost or gained due to your setback? For example, a lost job has all kinds of bright sides: exploring new job prospects, maybe even a new field. There's job hunting, which might not be all that much fun, but there's also in-person networking with new people at career fairs, group meetups, and free time to learn something new, catch up on some things at home, or sort out what your next moves will be. Never underestimate how important it can be to use your time wisely!

Now, go back and fill in the middle space with the things you CAN do now *because* of the setback, based on what you lost and gained. If it helps, try thinking of three MAIN goals or things you would like to change about your present that you can work on right now. For example, if my setback is a divorce, three main goals I might have are:

- Finalizing the divorce paperwork/legalities
- Building a Better Me with my newfound free time
- Getting my finances in order to help to meet my new responsibilities

Think about how the changes caused by the setback can be repurposed to propel you toward those goals.

I'll wait for you. *Humming the Jeopardy song*

Done? You sure? Ok, great. Even if you are not, you can go back to it if you need to. The idea here is that when you are ready, you can repurpose this empty space, which is an ability you may not have discovered for yourself before now. It may not have been the blessing you were looking for, and it may not feel or look like a blessing at all, but there is a blessing in EVERY empty space, lesson and set back – it is just up to you to identify it, adjust accordingly, and keep moving forward!

Part III – Acquire

Seven

THE WORK

So you've gone over and over what you've lost, and what you have now, and you FINALLY want to move forward. You're tired of sitting where you are, in the grief. In the pity party. You are over it already. You're dying to reorganize your life and rebound from the setback that caused you to buy this book in the first place! This is the WORK. This is the part of the book where I break down *how* to find the motivation to get UP, and *how* to apply basic goal setting to plan where you want to get TO.

Quick review:

- We've covered **acceptance**, in that we have discussed how to process and take inventory of what we lost, acknowledging those feelings and effects (mental and physical), and working through them in healthy ways.
- Then we discussed the present, **assessing** what we can use in our favor and want for our future, acting on the goals that will propel us to where we want to be.

My dad used to say the easiest path from point A to point B is a straight line. I am sure he did not make it up, but he would often use the truths of science to explain life. I did not understand it at the time, but applying it when I was older was the point of understanding for me. That's when I got it. I took that saying to mean that the best way to have something you want is to go after it, directly. It is almost always a waste of time to do something in a roundabout, halfway fashion because 9 times out of 10, you will wind up needing to eventually exert more effort to achieve your goal than if you just went for it directly. Figure out what you want and focus 100% of your efforts directly towards getting there – and you cannot help but at least get close to where it is you are trying to go.

For instance, my oldest son wanted to play tennis when he was about 5. He played with my mom a few times and loved it, but never after did he ask me – "Hey mom, can I play tennis as a sport?" Instead he asked about football, basketball, and soccer and then settled on mixed martial arts. My mother bought him a racket and he never played with it unless other people suggested it. I assumed he was just not as interested as he had expressed, you know how kids are, wanting something sooo badly…. for two seconds. He never brought it up again, so I assumed he lost interest. He is 12 now and has played football and currently competes in mixed martial arts tournaments. Randomly, I decided to enroll him into a two-week beginner's tennis class for the summer, remembering on a whim that it was something he enjoyed. When I told him about it, his whole face lit up, and he could not wait for the class to begin. Once the class began – guess who turned out to be a natural at tennis!! I mean, he is *really* good! He could have been taking classes all this time and be a semi-pro Olympian hopeful by now! Ok maybe not all of that. But still, he's great! I asked him why he did not say something about being interested in taking tennis classes or playing on a team; he shrugged, in that uninterested pre-teen kind of way, and admitted that he just did not think it was possible since no one he knew played tennis. Everyone he knew played football or basketball.

There are three points to this story. The first is, you are only limited by your own thinking – and that can be both a good thing and a bad thing. My son's mind was set on what he knew, which was that he liked playing but had no one to play with; so he gave up. His mind was limited at that point, screeching to a halt at the first closed door, which shut down any further action before he realized his potential. A five-year old does not usually have the reasoning skills to work around things after certain boundaries are set. If, in their minds, a door is locked, they usually move on to something else. (Now, retrieving a confiscated toy, or perhaps belly surfing down the steps to escape impending naptimes... *those* reasoning skills are a completely different matter!) As adults, however, we have learned to reason and we understand things are not always what they seem, especially with further exploration and experimentation. We know that sometimes, the door is just closed – not locked.

The second point: he had no action plan. We all have been in situations where if you have no goals or plans, time can slip by you in an instant – time you cannot get back. Sure, he was only 5 when he realized he liked tennis, and blame can also be placed on his parents, my husband and I, for not seeing his potential and planning for him sooner. But life does not always work that way. Time does not care who did not make the plan; it's going to pass by regardless. It is up to YOU to create your action plan, especially if you are not a five-year old, and you no longer have mommy and daddy planning your life for you. You have to put in the energy. The definition of energy is the ability to do *work*. (That's physics!) Your action plan is the WORK that moves you from point A to B. If there is no work done, no energy exerted, guess what? You will have no movement!

The third point is that environment is not always the most important factor; successful people can come from anywhere. But if you can create or place yourself in an environment that is conducive to your goals, it can make things 100 times easier. Justin never showed interest again after that first exposure to tennis. He never asked me in the following years for it seemed to never cross his mind. But once he was fully immersed in the environment, with other children his age who shared his other interests, instructors to help mold his technique, and constant practicing and goal setting among others with the same goals – he became a full-fledged tennis player. The potential was already there, the interest was already there, but the awakening and forward movement ONLY happened once he was in the right environment to put these ingredients to work.

The overall message? Align your **mindset, action plan,** and **environ-ment**, and you are bound to achieve your goals (or get from point A to point B) effectively.

Acquire the Mindset

Thinking positively is a good thing, and I'm sure that was what you thought I was going to say here. It is not—so there! What I'm going to say, is that acquiring something with the power of your mind, in my experience, has more to do with filling your head with <u>knowledge</u> about the subject of which you intend to be the master. In the case of my son and not being knowledge-able enough to know how to play, where to go, what groups were available to play with – the mindset was limited to: "*Want to play tennis. Can't because* ____. *(Insert excuses). Oh well.*" The end. Broadening your mind opens you to more than just new ideas – it opens doors to how you can *apply* your ideas.

If I dream of being a bilingual basketball coach, I need more than just a mean dribble and ideas on where to apply. I am going to need to start thinking of how to fill my arsenal with knowledge—so that no matter where I apply my skills, my chances of reaching and even excelling past my goals are darn near undeniable. I want to start purchasing books, taking language classes, sharp-ening my game, and asking as many experts as many questions as I can. The same goes with any goal. The things you want to change, the person you want to be now, after your set back, needs to be equipped with the right informa-tion needed to begin this new journey. Self-help books like this one, internet articles, and individual or group therapy will lead you to the tools you need – you just have to get your mind set on the options, get around like minded people, and focus on all roads that lead to your destination. Knowing all the roads helps you pick the shortest, straightest one!

There is a saying that goes,

As a man thinketh, so is he.

This is explained to mean that whatever you believe you are, you are. This is true when it comes to self-esteem and even when it comes to your limitations. One thing I want to note about this theory though is that you cannot rely simply on believing something hard enough. We cannot simply touch our temples and chant "belieeeeeeve" and make things true. ☺ Support is needed for any belief! Why? Well, if you are tested on that self-proclamation with a real life situation, without arming yourself with the proof that you are what you have believed, then merely *thinking* it is useless. If I thought I was the smartest person in the world and really believed it, just because, then as long as I remain unchallenged, that works. BUT if I am proved wrong with a real life situation, challenged by someone smarter – suddenly I am no longer what I believed. My believing it did nothing for my *reality* if I had only an opinion to support my belief. In my experience, if you support your belief by filling your mind with the proper tools to become what it is you believe yourself to be, you can back up your claims with facts. THEN when life tests you, you can back up your claims with facts. You may still not be exactly what you thought you were, but you will still probably be pretty close – and if you want, you can become it in reality – or get closer still by studying and mastering it.

Acquire the Environment

Being in the right PLACE at the right time is just as important as obtaining the tools you need to get a job done. Having the correct mindset is awesome, but it will not be as effective if your surroundings are not putting the mental tools to use.

After I performed an analysis of my past, took inventory of what I had in my present, and created my goals for the future, I believed I was ready to take action. One of my "Super Cool Mom" goals was to get back into shape so that I could learn a martial art form. I did the research online, created a list of things I needed to do to start my journey, but a few weeks went by and I was seeing no real changes. I was experiencing side effects from the new diet and fatigue from the new workout schedule, but not really experiencing any positive feedback for staying motivated to keep going. Sure, I had learned a lot about my body type and the new diets to try and the new workout moves I could do at home, but the motivation to keep pushing, being alone in my living room on my yoga mat, was just not there. I needed help! I needed to change my environment to one that included like-minded people with similar goals to help cheer me on or redirect my energy when I was feeling tired of experiencing plateau. I needed hands-on classes, with instructors to guide me toward the martial arts goals I wanted to achieve, connect with the best dojos in town, and to help me become a part of that community so that there was just no way to fail!

As a result of going to one tour of a recommended dojo, I learned that I could not only take classes, but the facility provided an aftercare service for my kids where while I was working out or taking my class, they would pick up the kids after school for me, train them in martial arts, AND provide homework help! As a new single parent juggling my full-time work schedule with personal goals and child care – I was SOLD! I made new friends and opened up a whole new world for myself, simply by putting myself in the environment I needed to be in to make the changes I wanted.

Eight

THE PLAN

I have developed the mindset, and found the environment to help me succeed, now what?

Acquire an Action Plan

The Law of Attraction

*The **law of attraction** is the name given to the term that "like attracts like" and that by focusing on positive or negative thoughts, one can bring about positive or negative results.*[3]

If you Google "The Law of Attraction," you will find a definition very similar to the one above as well as other information. The first time I read about it, I thought The Law of Attraction was going to be about the obvious: attracting people that were of like intentions or attracting to yourself what you want, by being around what you want; not exactly. It is actually a slightly different, more *internally* focused, concept. Put more simply, whatever you give out in

---

3 "Law of Attraction." *Wikipedia*. Wikimedia Foundation, n.d. Web. 09 Aug. 2015.

Thought, Word, Feeling, and/or Action, it is returned to you; more like the concept of Karma, with good or bad deeds. Whether the return is negative or positive, failure or success, you are in control. What you "speak" into the universe is what you get back. Many authors and celebrities such as Wayne Dyer, Oprah Winfrey, Will Smith, Jim Carrey, Steve Harvey, Rhonda Byrne, and many others, have testified to this 'amazing' Law of Attraction. But before we go into our cross-legged yoga pose and start chanting, let's really examine this on an everyday level, instead of the "speak to the universe genie and it shall grant you wishes" approach, shall we?

On a more logically balanced playing field, I think The Law of Attraction can be more easily understood and better accomplished by taking ownership of the close relations between what you want, what you *say* you are going to do about it, and what you *actually* do about it. We all know there are things we say that we would like to do, are going to eventually do, wish we could do, etc., that never actually get done. Wishing them into existence in these cases, with no actions to follow the words, usually falls upon deaf "universe genie" ears. However, when we follow those words with an action to put the deed into motion, then the universe's hearing perks up! Then we actually see some part, if not all, of our intentions take shape and begin to exist in real life where once they were just ideas in our minds. Now, there is nothing new about this concept. What I have to share is my experience *using* this concept for the specific purposes of moving forward from a negative to a positive position in my mind AND in real life.

When I was struggling every day through depression, grieving, crying, and praying myself to sleep, the last thing I wanted to hear was that I can "wish" my way to a better me by telling the "universe" what I want. I was like, what? Um no, I believe in God, not the universe genie. I never obtain a sense of wellness by simply wishing things were better and saying I am going to do better. DOING what I want to do to become better – that is what has rendered me results. The problem was, and I have seen that this is the case 9 times out of

10 with people who are depressed or going through some stage of loss, they do not know WHAT to DO to receive or accomplish what they want.

The process of figuring out how to transition from 'wanting to receiving' was grueling and time consuming for me. The first thing I did was get discouraged and I gave up. I do not recommend that path, for obvious reasons. I had made a list of the things I wanted to accomplish after dreaming up in my mind's eye the details of every little thing: each angle of life I wanted to tackle from my new profession, new workout regimen, and affirmations, all the way down to the color of the shoes I would wear during my motivational speeches I would be making from somewhere someday. Yet, despite all my precise planning, I had committed no *action* to these goals. There they were, on a great goal poster in my room, doing nothing but reminding me of what I had not accomplished yet. I had hit a wall. It depressed me more, so I mostly slept and surfed the Internet. Like all day. It was pretty pitiful. But it was my process, so I cannot be angry at the world or myself. I am also not one for pity parties, so the feelings of defeat motivated me better than any positive coaching ever could. Eventually, I did begin to have spurts of motivation and I managed to do a bit of reading with the Internet surfing. What I found in the mountain of old personal development books Jason and I had read together, years ago, between the lines of rhetoric and clever, but impractical clichés, there was more. Among the repetition of the same five to twenty steps to being productive, achieving goals, winning friends, or just being frickin' awesome – I noticed there was a basic pattern of about three things. There, in plain sight, were three *real* steps that kept popping up in each and every book and article.

So, guess what? I will save you the time. The three steps are:

1.   Write your MAIN goal down. Be VERY specific.

We have actually already begun that process! Hooray! Somewhere between the Acceptance and the Assessment portions of this book, you have talked about who you used to be, who you are now, and who you want to be, AND you were SUPER specific. You detailed all kinds of things you have going for you, thought of your next possible moves, and listed the main things you want to change– you are all set there! (And if not… get cracking!)

The carrot on the stick is what the horse wants; not so much to win, just to eat the carrot!

The reason you want to be very specific is because we are motivated by things that are tangible more so than things that are not, and we are driven farther by emotions that are strong versus those that are fleeting. What do I mean here? We know what our favorite flavor of ice cream tastes like and are quite familiar with the emotion we experience when that first taste hits our lips. We know the smell, the texture, the color, and exactly what a double scoop with extra toppings looks like! If this ice cream was a reward for something comparable, say cleaning your room or burning 500 calories in your workout today, most people would be so excited about the idea of the reward, the motivation to finish comes easily! You would definitely finish faster and stronger than you would have if there were no reward or a reward of something fleeting and intangible like "satisfaction." When we set goals for ourselves, especially goals that no one is keeping score for, where no one is competing with you, and where no one is cheering you on, the motivation tends to wane unless you have some reward hovering over your head. This reward needs to be as vivid in your mind as that ice cream. You need to be able to experience it, with all five senses, (sometimes it helps to actually be around that thing or someone who has what you want!) so that it is stuck in your mind's eye as the prize ahead.

For me, one of my main goals were was to be successful in spite of my grief, anxiety and new very time limited schedule. Even thought that sounds pretty targeted, I had to be *more* specific than that. What was success to me? I wanted to be a writer. Ok, write what about what? What will your first book be about? What will you be wearing, how will your hair look, and what will the perfume be that you wear the day you see your first book in print? Will you cry? Will you scream and jump around? Will it come in the mail? Where will you go to celebrate? Who's going with you? THESE specifics are what drove me during the lazy times when I was too tired to write, reschedule the writing goals when the kids needed help with homework. Even when I doubted myself or thought my work was not good enough, these images, burning in my head like a craving are what kept me going. My hands itched to touch my book cover. I could already feel the tears welling up when I thought about how I would feel, seeing it for the first time. I would catch myself daydreaming about shopping for Burberry cologne… because I needed to pick out my new scent for the day my book came! It really does work. Give it a shot!

2. Execute Daily Goals: Listing

Over and over in each book, I kept seeing this…and it gave me a little flutter inside. First the ADHD kicked in: *Okay, one thing a day, I can do that. I can do two…or three? What was I doing again? I keep forgetting everything!* That is when the anxiety would flare. *But where to start? I have too many things in my life to fix and not enough time in a day… Ahhhhhh*!!! That made room then for the OCD to try to organize things …. that is where the real fun began.

In case you are a person like me, who is easily overwhelmed by tasks with limited time and manpower, lists help out A LOT. Throughout my entire healing journey, I broke down my main goal into several smaller goals and compiled them into lists, sticky notes, and task boards. Now, as a habit, I create small lists just about every day. The joy that comes from crossing something off a list – fabulous!

Since I had lost the person I had built my old life with, on, and around, it was only logical to me to start a new life. I am not saying everyone should start from scratch whenever you lose someone or something major, you could start much smaller and just get a new goal, start a new routine, or adopt a pet! This was just *my* way of coping. First – I had to get out of my parent's house. I needed a new home since I did NOT want to go back to living in my old one where everything reminded me of my husband. For that I needed a new job, needed to figure out what to do with the current home (to sell or to rent), needed to get a financial advisor…where would I live… schools… money… the million thoughts I had that spiraled from the ONE idea of taking the first step to heal was SO overwhelming!

Here is where listing came in handy. Using three main things I wanted to change about my situation, I listed smaller, more detailed tasks needed to achieve each goal.

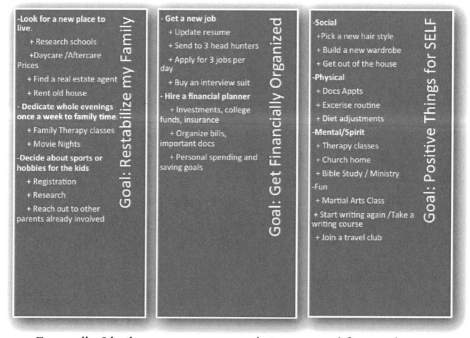

Eventually, I built my way up to completing one goal from each category every day. Before I knew it, I was attaching appropriate due dates to each goal per category and performing them in order. But that will come in time; as you begin to notice your own progress, you will begin to want more. Mastering the art of setting goals and scaling them down into smaller more achievable tasks is an invaluable technique! I felt accomplished and productive knowing I had taken at least one step toward my future … every day.

3. Stay Motivated

It is easy to start something new, but how do you keep the ball rolling? After making your lists and dreaming big things, you may have already felt the thoughts of doubt creeping in. You may have already thought of two or more excuses or "reasons" why you cannot set and achieve a goal each day. You are already rationalizing that maybe a goal a week sounds better? Know that this is ok! You are not defective or hopeless; you are human! Successful people are human too, so they have the same thoughts. The difference between success and failure? Motivation. You can't fail if you don't quit!

Motivation is about continuing long after the excitement has passed. The only way to do that is to tap into something that the brain will *believe*. As I have shared in this book, we can lean on our Core Beliefs to motivate us when we are down. We can access our arsenal of knowledge and experiences as logical support from the goal oriented mindset we created. We can go to our environment for support from other people who have achieved the goals or are facing the same bumps in the road as you. We build ourselves a failsafe around our goals because they are just as intangible and fragile as dreams and thoughts. We have to create them, act on them, and protect them from negativity and obstacles to get to where we dream of being.

So that is it! 1. Writing your goals down and being specific, 2. Executing daily goals, and 3. Staying motivated were the three main steps repeated in just about every goal setting, motivational and personal development book I've ever read (and I've read quite a few!) about setting and reaching goals successfully. Do not get me wrong; there were definitely many other valuable nuggets in the books I read. On this particular subject of setting and completing a goal, however, these seemed to be the steps that mattered.

Nine

WHO DO YOU WANT TO BE NOW?

Susan, my therapist, asked me one day,

> *"So when you meet people for the first time, what does your intuition tell you that they think? What does your body language say? What do you want them to take away from meeting you and how would you like to be treated thereafter? What do you want the description of your life from here on after your loss?"*

Well, actually, I didn't really know the answers to these questions. The thing that kicked me about what she was asking was it sounded like I had a choice! In retrospect, this sounds obvious; but have you ever wanted to be something, yet felt like your circumstances just would not allow it? I would love to be 22 again and hang out all night, but the reality of being a single parent means I'll more likely be on the couch with the kids accepting my PG rated movie night. What she was saying blew my mind because I had already decided that my loss was the end of all the *good* choices. My mind had allowed my loss to dictate the future and I was convinced it would be bleak and miserable trying to figure out how to move on or just replace what was my only known path to happiness. With the suggestion that I could shape this loss into a new LIFE, she had opened a small corner of my imagination to a whole new ball game.

She then said,

> *"Build it, look at it from all angles, and then **be** it. Learn it. Find people that live it and be their friend! Do whatever it takes to be whatever you want people to assume about you, to get from your actions, whatever you can create in your mind, you can be. You just have to decide WHO that is. The old Maya was one way. You have changed, and grown, and cannot fit her life anymore. WHO will you be NOW?"*

It just clicked to me. I knew almost immediately. I made a list of the things I wanted to accomplish and do and have in order to be the "new Maya," the "successful, great mom, loving life, moving forward Maya." Just like that.

I listed and created doodles about martial arts, singing, dancing, learning languages, financial organization and freedom, writing, and being a better mom; details like the clothes I would wear, the hairstyle, the fragrance, and the job title—all of it!

My mind began racing… and my patchwork quilt of "the New Maya" began its first square. Seeing this twinkling in my eye, that she had inspired something, she began to give me more "patches" to work with. She asked me to detail this new person that I would by asking a series of questions, which I have paraphrased for have paraphrased for below. So now, you try them!

Phase Four: Future Goals

Scratch Pad

Describe the physical things you want to be. Details!! What does "better you" LOOK like? What traits?

_____

_____

_____

_____

_____

_____

_____

_____

_____

_____

What are you wearing? On which day of the week do you have the best day of your new life? What did you eat for breakfast, lunch, and dinner? (Yes – THAT specific!)

_____

_____

_____

_____

_____

_____

_____

_____

_____

_____

_____

What do you want people to say about you and your situation after it's all over? Who do YOU want them to see you as? A survivor? A victim? A fighter?

_____

_____

_____

_____

_____

_____

_____

_____

_____

_____

_____

What 10-second pitch would you like to give to describe who you are, what you do, and where you are going in life, when you meet new people?

_____

At first I thought, (like you were probably thinking just now) "Now wait. I cannot just BE anything now, I have limits." This is true. Here is where you incorporate your positives list from the exercise in the Phase Two assessment. Your list of the good things you have going for you in your life may broaden your spectrum on what is possible EVEN inside your limits. For example, when Susan asked me how I wanted to "introduce myself," my mind's eye took me to the biggest dream first—a writer. BUT, immediately the limitations popped into my head: I am a single parent now, I do not have a job anymore, I might as well look for another job as a computer technician… that is where the money is; the *last* thing I can go be is a 'starving artist' or start from the bottom of some publishing company or even finish the writing course I had started before my life's rug had been ripped from under me. Sound like you? This is the type of thinking that was keeping me depressed and stagnant. I could not really move forward in this line of thinking because I was already defeated. I had defeated myself! When I protested and gave her my spoken dissertation as to why what I *wanted* to be did not matter, she told me something I will never forget, and have made it into a bit of a mantra that I use every day now whenever I come across a barrier or limitation. It is this:

Speed limits don't stop forward movement.

You can stay inside the speed limit and still go fast because "fast" is relative. More simply put: You can stay inside your limit and still get what you want! Within your limits, how much of what you want *could* you have? How can you utilize your strengths to get what you want REGARDLESS of your limits?

That mantra changed my mindset completely. She then asked me to envision this writer—this single mom writer, maybe a single mom writer who works full-time as a computer technician. *Specifics* were the key. How specific could I make this goal, this new me? How could I tailor it to be attainable and feasible according to MY boundaries, but still catering to MY strengths?

I once heard that when you are envisioning something, you have to be detailed. I was—down to the hair! I pictured – now don't ya'll laugh at me – being Joan, from "Girlfriends." Natural hair, awesome style, and just all around "on point". Later, I incorporated an amazing young natural hair blogging guru named "Curly Nikki" into my patchwork quilt of "beings." I added a little bit of Oprah, because I wanted to be a social genius with lots of different streams of success – and I wanted to be smart about my money. Add a dash of my mother, to ensure that I would be the best mother to my kids imaginable and be able to balance an awesome career at the same time, and lastly, I wanted to be like Elizabeth Swann, from *Pirates of the Caribbean*. Ok, you can laugh at that one. I just wanted to be physically fit, be cool, and be a lady at the same time. I wanted to have interesting, nontraditional qualities, and be able to kick butt if I needed to!

Look back through the details you provided in your answers just now. Who is in your "patchwork quilt of beings"? What (realistic) happy ending do you envision yourself having? Who is your hero? Does anyone's story inspire you? Any movie characters, no matter how silly? I won't tell! ☺ Your imagination is your creative engine! Put some fuel in it and give it some direction, you'll be amazed where it leads you!

Ten

PUTTING IT ALL TOGETHER

*A*nd that brings us very near to the end of my story. This is where I leave you to use what you've learned to act on <u>your</u> decision to begin again. You are not alone in the struggle back to "normal", but you are now way ahead of some people who are experiencing the same hopeless feeling that made you purchase this book. Things happen. Life keeps on truckin', with or without you. But now, when life whacks at you with its big ol' change stick, be it a slight tremor or the big one - *you* have a strategy for coping, evaluating and rebuilding yourself and finding the peace that comes with knowing without any doubts that you really will "be OK".

Let's recap the main three steps:

- **Accept the pain, grief and setback.** We talked about accepting your reaction, and how to accept the help you might need to pull through the initial emotional responses.
- **Assess what you're working with.** We discussed how to take inventory of what you had/were, what you have/are now, and what you want/want to be. I also showed you how to use that inventory as the main tool for your next moves.

- **Acquire the means to be better than you started**. We analyzed our inventory to create an action plan, we learned how to set the goals, and most importantly, how to stay motivated.

It all sounds so easy right? One thing I won't do in this book is lie to you, paint pretty pictures of beach silhouettes in the sunset, and tell you to expect an overnight miracle. Did this process work for me? Yes. Is it going to work for you? It can. Did I have setbacks and pitfalls? Of course. If your loss was so great that you felt the need to purchase a book about getting past it: "easy" was probably not the expectation. You're definitely smarter than that.

What I will tell you, is once you have gone through these steps, and you feel you're ready, you will be better. You will also have more questions. I definitely don't have all the answers. *What!?* If you thought once you finished this book you were going to know it all, have all you ever needed, and start levitating…Nope. Life doesn't work that way either. (But please call me if you *do* start levitating, in which case I would need to charge MUCH more for this book! Kids gotta eat! I'm a single parent! *Wink*) Seriously though, after you have become mentally and physically back on track, and after you have set goals and start seeing some results, you'll probably wonder what is next. Will you still miss the piece of your life that is gone, now that you've found a way to move on? Will this new way of living and new goal of becoming better than you were before the loss make you happy? Will you finally be at peace? I honestly don't know.

That is where I am now. Sometimes I am sad and miss my late husband. I look through old pictures, old emails I have kept, and talk to trusted friends about good times, and maybe even cry a little (With a LOT of tissues!). Thankfully, I'm through the worst of the mourning, I believe, and most of the time I am very happy! I look around my life and see all that has come about, all that I have accomplished, and all that I have to look forward to. And to me, there is much more balance. I think I will always miss Jason, until the day I die. I do not think anyone should be made to believe they have to forget about their losses in order to get over their losses. "Getting over it" has nothing to do, in my experience, with moving on. I know people who still harbor feelings about losing a job, or losing a friendship, or losing a health battle – and these losses serve as motivation for them. It serves as a lesson learned or pivotal life experience that they would not trade for the world once they got through it. For some people, the clarity that comes with loss is essential to their growth. For some, it is excruciating, but it opens their lives to something they would not have had, had they not made room for it. Loss is just one of those things: it can be unbearably hard to live with it, but you definitely can't live without it. The good news is loss is like a hole in your heart that can be filled with other things. Yes, the hole will still be there, but the new things inside it, new adventures, new experiences, new triumphs, those can live inside that space.

We all get tempted, too, as time creates a space between us and 'ground zero', to try to take new things and create the same old life we had. One thing I learned is that this does not lead to happiness. I learned the hard way that you have to fully accept that something is gone in order to fully enjoy what replaces it. I also learned that this replacement cannot only be "a place holder;" it has to be a new adventure entirely. It cannot be bound by the same rules, conditions, comfort zones, or expectations that the old life had. For example, I cannot date a new man expecting him to be Jason. I cannot get a new job expecting it to be the one I lost. I cannot be angry if I am not treated the exact same way, or expect to be happy about the same things, or demand that a new husband or potential new job measure up to the same expectations I had with the old ones. I'm not saying I needed to lower my PERSONAL standards. I believe there are many vehicles, but only one path to happiness for each person and everyone needs to have their basic needs met in order to find it. I am say-ing that I had to learn to be open to different interpretations of love or situa-tions that successfully meet my basic needs --and do *my* part to be sure I can be happy with them – not measure them by comparison to what I had before. In other words, novelty does not make you happy. Replacing old things with new things that look, and smell, and act just like the old things… it is not going to make you happy. Being at peace with knowing that no matter what comes next, you can do YOUR part to ensure YOUR level of happiness, YOUR goals are met, and YOUR successes are up to par – that is what can make YOU a happy person, regardless of what comes your way.

The part where I "bounced back better" was never about forgetting the past or replacing what I lost. It was about using the past as a springboard to move forward and change my trajectory. Yes, losing my husband threw me for the biggest loop of my life – but it was up to ME to decide where I landed, and in which direction I would get up and start walking again. Bouncing back was about taking a look at the empty space I had in my heart, and instead of being sad about the space; finding inner peace with two facts:

1. That empty space, after healing, is simply a new place to fill. I have the power to dust myself off and fill it all over again.
2. Nothing lasts forever, bad things included.

Eleven

CHANGE AIN'T GOIN' ANYWHERE

Six years later, I am *still* not perfect, but I am definitely at peace. This whole situation, the changes I went through and whether I would change anything about it knowing now where it would eventually lead me.... I feel like, perhaps there are two sides to every loss. On the one hand, I loved my husband more than anything. I miss what I lost, terribly. Our marriage was happier than any other marriage, like ever—to us, anyway. In our minds, other relationships seemed so imbalanced and unhappy, while ours was a miracle. We did the dumbest things and had a blast. We danced when there was no music, skipped hand-in-hand in parking lots, and dared each other to yell "helloooooo!" out the car window to people driving by. We were just plain crazy in love. He knew the real me. The Maya that whined daily about my post-partum tummy, bit the "butts" off French fries instead of eating them, and left a trail of clothing and clues wherever I had been. He knew the person that drooled in her sleep, could not cook, and had never balanced (or had) a checkbook before meeting him. And he loved me—really, really loved me. Who knows why? Hell, I do not know; just got lucky, I guess. And I was angry that I had to give that up.

But the other side of it is there are so many things that I AM NOW because of that turn of events. Because he showed me how to be loved, gave me my children, showed me what a good man really looked like, I am so much better. I am a better person from just witnessing his existence. I am a better mom because of my dual experience of being a mother in both a double and a single parent home, and perhaps one day will be a better wife because of the experience of being married to him. My dreams are now at the forefront of my life and finding the guts to carry on passed such a poignant struggle has been the key motivator for me to act on them. Without this dramatic shift, without some drastic change in my life, I do not know that I would have ever been pushed hard enough to get here.

Change is like that. That is what it does. It shakes things up, snatches the warm fuzzy rug right out from under you, and you have to react! You can keep sitting there, on the bare floor and wait for your rug to come back. You can hate change and lament the loss. You can grieve and cry and throw yourself an entire "missing fuzzy rug" pity party. I will happily volunteer to help you make the milk carton signs!

But you cannot stay there. When you are ready, you need to know you *have* to move forward. You cannot live in the past; there is no room. *Your present and future are happening now; they cannot fit in your life if you live with your memories.* And just in case you thought you could avoid change's next visit… think again! Change ain't goin' anywhere. Whether you ignore it, hate it, love it, embrace it, or constantly trip over it—it will keep coming back to pry the new fuzzy rug right up from under you, faster than you can super glue it to the floor.

Well, what am I supposed to do, then?! How can I be happy knowing that change is going to eventually come? I am glad you asked. This is the same lesson I had to learn.

You keep your happiness in the moments; live your life, moment to moment. If you have a bad moment, move forward to the next one. Decide what that moment is going to have in it! You keep planning your days, even if it might rain – because sometimes it will not. You keep dreaming up new dreams, even if they do not pan out, because some of them WILL. You keep living your life, even if it is the last day – because no matter what happens, you only get one chance to LIVE. Just like the story I shared earlier in the book about the King who looked for the secret to eternal peace, *there is peace in knowing that change is always coming.* If there are clouds gathering to signal a storm coming or if there is sunshine peeking through to end the darkest of days, either way, knowing that nothing lasts forever and being mentally armed with resilience - being prepared for <u>whatever</u> comes next: that is the way to finding peace. Knowing that whichever way the wind blows, you know how to open your sails and ride it, or rebuild your boat from scratch if you need to - that is inner peace to me. No one is perfect, and we all have to be reminded of these things from time to time, but if you can depend on nothing else, know that the only thing that is constant is change. I'd heard that saying a million times, but definitely had to really dig deep and figure out what that meant for me in my loss.

The two minds about it- the tug of war between the love left behind with the struggle to find enough love for myself and knowing I am a success story before I even finished this book – that is my inner peace. How can a war bring peace? Well, it is not pretty. But after all that pain, depression, and anxiety, I did not witness any miracles, life went on, and nothing or no one spectacular came out of the sky to grant me any wishes or glass slippers – but I still can claim victory because the outcome is a new me. It may not have been forged the way I would have preferred, but, like they say, diamonds are not made out of plastic – they are made with high heat and intense pressure; from hard, solid rock.

It really has taken fire and hell to bring me out, renewed. God has shown himself present in that, I still have my mind intact, my will to move forward, and my dreams ahead of every new footstep. I am now living proof of the things I've read in books, seen in movies, and heard from someone's uncle's cousin's brother: ***Despite it all, you can definitely bounce back. You can come out of ANY thing, and <u>make the decision</u> to be better.***

Made in the USA
Middletown, DE
02 October 2015